THE SUBALTERN SPEAK

YESHWANT NAIK

Copyright © Yeshwant Naik
All Rights Reserved.

This book has been published with all efforts taken to make the material error-free after the consent of the author. However, the author and the publisher do not assume and hereby disclaim any liability to any party for any loss, damage, or disruption caused by errors or omissions, whether such errors or omissions result from negligence, accident, or any other cause.

While every effort has been made to avoid any mistake or omission, this publication is being sold on the condition and understanding that neither the author nor the publishers or printers would be liable in any manner to any person by reason of any mistake or omission in this publication or for any action taken or omitted to be taken or advice rendered or accepted on the basis of this work. For any defect in printing or binding the publishers will be liable only to replace the defective copy by another copy of this work then available.

Contents

Author's Note

This book is a work of art. It encourages readers to consider prose, poetry, opinions, and thoughts as art because there are many similarities. Each of these works draws the eye to the depth and action like a sculpture or painting. Reading this book is like walking through a museum. The reader's imagination will help him to form a picture.

This book is a work of art. It encourages readers to consider prose, poetry, opinions, and thoughts as art because there are many similarities. Each of these works draws the eye to the depth and action like a sculpture or painting. Reading this book is like walking through a museum. The reader's imagination will help him to form a picture.

The book is a compilation of the voices of subaltern, marginalized Others (gay men and transgender persons). Their proclivities, opinions, and thoughts are captured in their own words.

When we read fiction, we see the world through the eyes of a character. It is impressive to see how a character interacts with the world around them. The beauty of literary fiction is in the reader's understanding and perception and how they will live their lives in accordance with the lesson reflected in the story.

The book presents the lived experiences of the subalterns in the form of opinions, thoughts, poem, monologues, illustrations, humor, and conversations recorded during the sub-project "Homosexuality in the Jurisprudence of the Supreme Court of India," which is part of Cluster Project A2-7 "Pluralism and the Justification of Norms in Modernity" (Cluster of Excellence Religion and

Politics, University of Münster). The book explores some physical and virtual forum interactions of the community members. Each of these conversations has a deep message to convey. Few free images from the internet are used.

This raw literature, consisting of unpublished field notes, was part of the ethnographic fieldwork in 2015. Part of the text is in Hindi; I have provided an English translation.

I thank my Professors for giving me the opportunity to work on this project. I thank my family and friends who encouraged and supported me to make this book a reality. I hope that readers will gain a better understanding of the problems and challenges faced by LGBTQ+ persons in India.

Introduction

On September 6, 2018, India's Supreme Court legalized consensual homosexual sex. The court's decision overturned part of a 19th-century law, introduced by the British and known as Section 377, that made sex "against nature" a crime punishable by life imprisonment. Almost four years after this law was passed, what is the status of LGBTQ+ rights in India? Can these subalterns speak? Although the Supreme Court ruling was limited to decriminalizing consensual homosexual sex, it has spurred a positive discourse on gender and sexuality in the public sphere without fear of reprisals from the authorities.

Parliament passed the Transgender Persons (Protection of Rights) Act, 2019, but it does not allow for self-determination of transgender status. The law does not provide for reservations in public employment and education, as required by the Supreme Court ruling. Therefore, the law is being challenged in the Supreme Court.

In India, it's not just about the law. An entire culture contributes to making homosexuality a taboo. There is no comprehensive anti-discrimination law. The constitution prohibits discrimination, but the prohibition applies only to the government and its organs. The private sector is exempt from the ban in the areas of employment, health, housing, and education. There is no political consensus on passing an anti-discrimination law. The courts are inactive. In the absence of data, the problem becomes even more serious.

Although there is no comprehensive movement against discrimination against the queer community, voices in support of those discriminated against are growing louder. People have begun to realize that something needs to change. There is acceptance in the media and in Bollywood. Several queer films have been released. Television channels, social media, and newspapers have often spoken positively against Section 377. But not all media platforms have been tolerant. Some are still indifferent to the issues facing the queer community. Nonetheless, new media has increased the interpersonal visibility of LGBTQ+ individuals and made them more likely to come out and be open about their identities to friends, neighbors, and co-workers. Today, companies that openly support LGBTQ+ rights are benefiting from this trend.

Facebook and other private online forums provide important spaces for Indian LGBTQ+ communities to find solidarity, advice, and partners. Many such forums existed long before the country's Supreme Court decriminalized same-sex sexual activity in 2018. Being part of these forums made them feel less lonely. It helped them talk to others about their problems and life experiences. Many still feel excluded even within the community due to their low social status and various other reasons. But unlike the 1980s and 1990s, these subalterns can speak today. The queer community alone cannot make a significant social impact. Therefore, it is important to seek alliances so that the voices of the subaltern are properly heard. As citizens, we have a responsibility to stand up against injustice.

1

Identity

"Our identity is exactly that we do not know that we construct our identities and still say that identity is illusion or imagination."

"Let's say we have consciousness, and the cockroach does not. If that's so, does it make us 'better', more important or whatever? No, that's just our specific lie. A result of circumstances – the genes we were born with, the surroundings, we grew up I would say the cat has turned into an activist."

"Don't accept the lies of the groups, make up your own (Obviously, I am doing the same....) On a deep level... it does not matter."

"The deal with most Indian men is identity crisis. They start off being straight men having sex with men, then bisexuals and finally gay."

"Creating a silly imitation of straight society is... too idiotic, really. There isn't any solution since the foundation is based on false premises. The dreamers who try to create perfect society are one of the main reasons why there never will be one."

2

Categorising

"Why do people still categorise humans. Yeah, I have been asked that before even 'is field mein kab se ho'? (Since how long are you in this field) And I have to ask, field? You mean architecture? No, and they say, 'nahin is line mein'(no in this occupation).

"Main toh is line mein Jab se paida hua tab se hu. Lekin saala aaj tak kisi ne koi 'payment' nahi diya. (I am in this field since my birth but I didn't receive any payment till date)."

3
Community

"Sometimes I use the term, 'within the community' but then I realise kaun se community? It almost sounds like we are a 'cult, a brother or sisterhood'. I wouldn't object to the usage of the word 'community' though."

"Most common words used for gay people, like gud, mittha, dheela, fail to convey the meaning. In fact, these are just derogatory words that aim to emphasise how un-manly most gay men are."

"Yahaan pe aise bahut log hain jo shadi shuda hone ke baawjood bhi apne app ko single ya hardcore gay bataate hain …. aaj jo log bisexuals ko condemn kar rahe hain, many of them will succumb to pressures and get married eventually … (There are many married men who claim to be single and gay, today those bisexuals who condemn gays, many of them will succumb to pressure and eventually get married)."

"Maata pita ko khush rakhne ke chakkar me Wife ki watt laga dete hain. (To make parents happy, they ruin the life of their wives)."

4

Tolerance

"India is a much better place for homosexuals. Indians by nature are very tolerant. However, their tolerance lies in their ignorance about facts. Try walking hand in hand or hand on shoulder of another man in Utah or Alabama, and then see how Americans cut your b-lls."

5

Hairdresser

"If you read the newspaper today, the media have not written, 'A Hairdresser was killed', it used the term 'A Gay hairdresser was killed by his Friend'. We still are fighting for our rights, and such incidents do not help the cause. Someone got robbed and murdered, this happens a lot every day."

"We are not stories, nor do we exist to make stories for you to report. Being gay is not pepper and salt."

"A criminal is a criminal, whether gay or straight. Does straights blame all of them for all the str8 thieves, murderers, dacoits?"

Humor

"When will you marry???
When the time comes
When will that time come?
When I will marry.... ek din kar lo (one day get married) ... people will stop asking, dusre din talak de do (divorce the next day) ... people will start asking again because they have no other work."

"Mujhe aaj hi hamari padosan ne poocha, Laddoo kab khila rahe ho? (Today my neighbour asked me, when will you give me Laddoos (sweets)?

I replied, 'Aunty, jab aap bolo tab (Aunty whenever you request)'.

She said, 'Aise nahi, shaadi wale Laddoo (Not just laddoo, I want laddoos from your marriage)'.

I replied, 'kya fark padta hai Auntyji, shaadi wala hoy aa bina shaadi wala, matlab toh sirf laddoo se haina (what's the difference Auntyji, marriage Laddoos or other laddoos, means the same, Laddoos are laddoos (sweets are sweets)'.

She said, 'very smart, Yeh who laddoo hai khaa kar pachhtana accha hai (they are those laddoos you should eat even if you have to repent).' I smiled."

7

Confusion

"Ek word main mujhe koi batata, Gay sex India main rahega yan ahi? (Can someone tell me in one word, will gay sex stay in India?)

What do you mean, rahega yan ahi??? (Stay in India?)

Gay sex koi NRI hai kay ki India me rahega yaa foreign country me rahega? (Is gay sex some Non-resident Indian to stay in India or to stay in a foreign country?)"

"Shahrukh ne khud ko gay accept kar lia to uske fan bhi kar lenge, aur kal ko Shahrukh mukar gaya to fans waapis straight ban jaaenge? … (If Actor Shahrukh accepts himself as a gay, his fans will also accept themselves as gays, and tomorrow if Shahrukh rejects himself, then will fans become straight again?)"

"Mom do you like Shahrukh Khan?

Yes, beta (son) I do.

Well, he is gay and so am I.

Oh, beta (son) because you told me about him, I am so proud of you, now you will become a super star too.

Why do people want celebrities to declare their sexual preferences when we ourselves cannot make all our own friends declare it and come open? Charity begins at home."

8

Motivation

"Since you are not a celebrity the society would take pot shots if ever. If God has not shown he is guilty of making you this way, then why should you feel bad at all? For you did not beg to come into this world. It is your life now and you have to adore yourself no matter what!"

9

"Yeah...lots of guys want sex without protection nowadays
   It's very dangerous
   but why it's happening?
   There might be 100 reasons...
   "We all desire things in life, but maybe differently. How are friends different from lovers to a relationship?"
   Do you think gay relationship will work in India? I guess only 2 to 5 % chances."
   "What is style in upper class is taboo in middle and is way of life in lower strata..and since we know in lower strata education and being 'classy' has got no place- earning and survival are the issues - safe sex isn't any consideration and is something to tease each other about!... people laugh when a man goes to buy a flavoured condom- kya ch--t strawberry khaati hai teri biwi ki? is a joke I heard few daily laborers laugh over with their fellow worker once!"

10

Marriage Pressure

"Was shocked to see so many celebrities as well as heterosexually married men are gays. The guy who I met was none other than my own manager in my office. I wish I was married to a man too. Hope society will soon change."

"Seeing my friends getting married to girls and having boyfriends at the same time really makes me wonder if my decision of not getting into marriage makes me stronger than them or weaker than them."

"Today someone made me realise how proud I should be for coming out to my sister and for choosing to follow my heart and not get married, for all those who think I am lucky to have accepting and understanding family, wait! It wasn't that easy. I had my share of trouble too. More than that, my family knows it is their turn to face the problems by facing our relatives and neighbours. This is however much better than destroying someone else's life."

"We all feel the need of someone in our lives and at times get into relationships to get over these insecure feelings. However, within the gay community I have seen blatant abuse of such relationships. While there are several couples, I know that have been together for 15, 18, even

20 years, there are many who have these two month and 3-month flings. What's scary is that when one gets into a relationship, safe sex is considered a no no since one has to prove faithfulness and integrity to the relationship. This has huge consequences. Also, many relationships are abusive, but people do not know how to get out. We can choose our relationships wisely and not rush into them to impress our friends or anyone else."

"I will be getting married soon
gaon ki ladki launga (I'll take a village girl)
khana banwaunga (I'll ask her to cook)
pair dabwaunga (I'll ask her to massage my legs)
aur agar usney zyada tein-tein ki tou
do chaar rakh bhi dunga (and if she starts nagging, I'll give her four slaps)."

"Our acceptance is conditional, 'we place society before us'. We give more importance to what others think, we love/fear society more than ourselves. We love/fear ourselves more than society."

"I think, people who don't follow their heart or get influenced by someone and go against their heart should think twice before taking any important decision related to their life if they have one..."

"...isliye hamesha gaadi kharidne se pehle test drive karo" (go for a test drive before buying a car).

"kabhi kabhi gadi thoda chal kar ruk bhi jati hai... ya doosre rastay par chalna shuru kar deti hai ....kitnay gays hain jinke khud ki aulaad bhi hai par ab wife ke siva sabse sex karte hain...."

"Sometimes a vehicle runs for a while and stops or starts running on another road... many gays have children and are now leaving aside wife they have sex with everybody."

maine kab kaha ki yeh gays and straights ka maamla hai? (When did I say that this is a gay or straight matter?) where did you get THAT? and why did you even think that the ENTIRE family was gay? .... All I am saying is that willfully cheating another person like that is sickeningly bad."

"Why does kundali (horoscope) matching for homosexuals does not exist in India?"

11

Desire

———♡———

"What is wrong about seeking a human desire called sex? Do you feel sex is a 'sin' and 'dirty'? Is seeking sex from willing partners 'indecent'?

What one portrays in public is not what one is in private. Human beings are masked."

"As far as loyalty in gayism goes, please don't expect any. Gays have not achieved a reputation of 'the faithful one', cause most gays cheat on their partners or dump them for new ones. Of course, you could be lucky to have an exception."

"No one is loyal here............my desire if for oasis .... never fulfilled.... failed in search my oasis..........duniya me 95% aur yaha par 100% log dhokebaj hote hai god bless them all ... (in society 95% and in community 100% people are betrayers)."

"I am looking for a guy with whom I can spend the rest of my life.........just joking.... I know it's not possible here in India.

I am not looking for six pack type guys or any hero type of guys but still jisko dekh kar kiss karne ka mann to ho, jisko dekh kar dil me ghanta baj jaaye (still the person who you see feel like kissing just by seeing him and by looking at him heart beats)."

"Jawani me tu dega nahi aur budhape me teri koi lega nahi abhi waqt hai dede jawani ka maza lele (when you are young you will not give and when you grow old nobody will take from you, this is the time to give and have fun when you are young)."

"What harm is done to the society by fucking around? I can understand killing is wrong but fucking around can't be wrong. A killer shouldn't get rights, but why shouldn't a polygamous single person get rights?"

"Law cannot enforce happiness. Law can only punish but cannot establish happiness or cannot make two people love each other... If Law had that power to make people love, do you think there would have been wars? Like you can take a horse to the water source, but you cannot make horse drink water, so is the case with Law and love. Law can punish you if you marry another person, but Law cannot blossom love in hearts of people. It can instill fear and hence it would govern. Darr ke balbute par pyaar nehi kiya jata, Samjhauta kiya jata hai" (On the base of fear you can't love, it can only be a compromise) Those who want to f-ck around will f-ck around with or without a law."

12
Stay Anonymous

The game of making and breaking
    Making castle of dream
    And breaking them with flood of tears
    Crumbling goes my dream
    Along the lines of my face
    A new line appears
    And so does a new dream
    Love exists.... when it is there for straights then it is surely there for gays also...

13

Monogamy

———❤———

"I do not agree with the society on this. I am fighting by being promiscuous. I don't care whether I get rights or not. There are already so many poor people who don't get anything in India. Marriage and monogamous commitment look like rewarding talents? I don't have them, and I don't want them."

"When we are born, we become separated from our mother. Then, our individual journey starts, there is no such thing as soulmate, our life is for to be happy in every moment, bringing smile on other faces is the biggest achievement of life, not to find soulmate. So, enjoy life, see green tree, see green garden, see nila akash (blue sky) that are only for you, see smile on kids, you will enjoy every moment of life."

"I have been in a steady relationship for some time. But it so happens that live-in culture doesn't exist here... especially for gays.... and people are scared to commit for lifetime. When you have pleasure of the world at your feet... why stick to one person... there is no ego and hatred etc., but its more promiscuity that leads to break ups, man is ultimately a horny creature!"

"I know men who have been in relationship for over 5, 10, 20 and even 25 years in relationship. Just that most men running after sex, the priorities have slightly changed."

"The fight for gay marriage has started in India. But it of course means getting legal rights like a heterosexual marriage and getting all the benefits what straight people get in terms of right over property and right to adopt a child as a couple. Don't mix it with the permission to have sex with anyone or being promiscuous. Promiscuity goes into the domain of morality. What's moral for you may not be moral for me or vice versa. Open relationship is okay for me since it's based on both guys agreeing to it, and neither are cheating on each other. Of course, I would personally not prefer to be in an open relationship. But wont judge who are in such a relationship. But no system legalises promiscuity. But if you are not cheating anyone by being promiscuous it's fine."

"License for prostitution is only for having sex to earn money. Whether you have it with a woman or man is not the concern. The licence for prostitution doesn't mention that the person can only have straight sex."

"Being promiscuous is about morality. And morality is always subjective. So, rest assured nothing will happen to the traditions and culture on that front.

Promiscuity has no legal binding. So, no one gets any legal permission to be promiscuous."

"A marriage is a relationship between two people. What understanding they want to have between them should not be decided by others or society or rules. Let them both together decide. If it's agreeable to both without any force, it's fine for me. None of your actions or decisions should create issues in general. It should remain between the two."

"Marriage is not about gender... it's about love..."

"If I start doing something that someone else is doing it, it means that even I had a secret desire of doing it. Just that I was afraid to do it till now. In that case where is the culture anyway?"

"Well.... why compare us with heterosexuals. What we need for ourselves, we have to try for it, whether we have more options like them or not."

"Ethics...No one knows what it is. All they go to is Ramayana. Almost everyone likes Lord Rama, and they take him as an ideal son, husband, and king. 'Eka patni vrata' is the golden standard with comparison to that dating 3 guys one after another is also unethical. Let's not judge guys who date others. Ethics do change from place to place and time to time."

"Ethics cannot and should not be imposed on anyone but oneself. My ethics will vary from the guy next to me. If I were in a relationship, I would not consider it unethical to have sex with other guys with the knowledge and approval of my partner. I will also not accept anyone's argument that it is unethical because that's their ethics which they are free to follow but they are certainly not free to impose those on me. Their ethics do not apply to me, only mine does."

"What exactly is convenience? Can it be termed as trying to lead our life the way we want to in the best and most comfortable manner possible? Are you saying, "the convenient way" and "the right way" are mutually exclusive? Who decided monogamy is a virtue? You? The society you live in? The same society that until recently said that homosexuals are abominations, in fact still does. The same society that until recently thought that keeping humans as slaves was not wrong at all? Did ethics play a role in changing those views of your society? If they did then can we say that those very ethics of the society changed over time as it became more open minded and realized that it needs to be more open minded? Let me say it again. I will not accept your morality or your ethics. I decide whether monogamy is a virtue for me. It is not a convenience. It is my right, and it is me. You can judge me all you want. That judgement doesn't make 'your wrong' 'my wrong'.'My right' may be 'your wrong' but I'm not imposing it on you."

"Major reason for society thinking homosexuality is wrong is because homosexuals have a lot of sexual partners? Please tell me you are joking. Have you seen how many straight men are not faithful to their partner sexually? Even after being married."

"Acceptance comes when one proves that what is happening in heterosexual society can happen in homosexual society too. I do not want what's happening in the heterosexual society to happen in the homosexual society. You may be needing society's approval for your life. I certainly do not. Who told you that I want the same thing that is happening in the heterosexual society? That I want that same kind of acceptance? See this is where you are so grossly wrong. Just because heterosexuals do something in a certain way does not make it right or make it something that I or many other homosexual guys want. Many do and many don't want that as well. The norms of society are ingrained into everyone's mental state so badly that anything or anyone going against them is considered wrong. That has been one of homosexuality's main obstacle as well. I do not need to prove anything to the heterosexual society."

14

Coming Out

"There are definitely a few couples who have been accepted by their families. And these days more and more guys are coming out to their families. And quite a few have been accepted by the parents if not the entire family."

"Most times it's not about the acceptance of something so different by the parents that matters. But it's about how much they are ready to accept for the happiness of their children. What makes them happier. ... their pride or their children's happiness.

Most parents accept them for the love of their children and not due to their broad mindedness but due to their big heart. Indian culture had led a lot of parents not to accept their sons as gays due to the shame factor. In such a case a lot of guys may feel it's better not to come out. It's totally their choice. They have to decide which is important to them .... Living a life of lie and always feel guilty or decide to come out and live a life of confidence and self-worth even if there is no acceptance from family."

"Adjustments are a part of life. If your parents accept you and don't force, you into a marriage then you also need to accept some of their wishes."

"Leave him alone…… his sexuality is his business… who are we to question?"

"Whatever talk is going on in the media, whether it is something that you like or not, but look at in this manner that, it's bringing the whole issue to public attention. Never was society in general aware of the existence of so many LGBT people in the community and the acceptance has also risen. If people like us won't come out in open and become ready to talk in the media that people like us also exist who don't talk only about sex or for whom being gay is not only about sex, but we will also have to remain content with those who are willing to come on TV and talk whatever they want. Things change only when people with opposing views come out in open and express their views. If we can't come out in people, then we have no right to raise our fingers on those who are out and speaking their mind."

"Homosexuality has been legalized in India only a few years ago and contrary to what we choose to believe a - High court order certainly doesn't change the nation, society or even a gay man used to of hiding himself all the time, overnight! it's not like high court says- Okay Gays are legal… and everyone gets up and announces - oh this is me, this is my pic and I am here for taking! contrary to what people from other countries don't understand - what takes years to accept and hide also takes years to come out."

"We all must understand that to get over fears of a trauma suffered in the past is not too easy. In India people find their own ways to deal with their traumas - unlike west not every third man is on the couch of a psychiatrist every few days. the social support system here is more community and family oriented. people here don't have to pay to look for support so with each 'pro' in the system comes a 'con'. tolerance and patience are an Indian virtue and a curse in certain cases."

"There are various reasons for people to hide their face within the community. Sometimes it is the fear of being found out by family or friend, sometimes it is fear of criticism from those who bluntly comment on one's appearance, sometimes it is fear of being exposed by some TV channel ...and usually people who are governed by the over cautious atmosphere that prevails in society where privacy is more a variant of the minds capability to handle insecurity of identity revelation. Anyhow, whatever the reasons behind it, nothing is sacrosanct. Causes of insecurity in India are very different from those that people face in western countries."

"Homosexuality, for many, is a stigma/taboo which will need more than mere acknowledgement from the Government. It needs cleansing of the minds of the thousands who think it is a disease. ....Back in the west, muggers and goons are considered bigger criminals than homosexuals whereas, in India, surprisingly, till date, there are scores who would consider a homosexual boy a bigger 'criminal' than a mugger."

15

Sarcasm

———❦———

"Indians ki saari Khushi aur saari pareshaani kewal sex se hi judi hui hai

Rape ho to pareshaani,

incest ho to pareshaani,

child abuse ho to pareshaani,

polygamy ho to pareshaani,

yeh sab to thik hai,

lekin Aish abhi tak maa kyun nahi ban rahi yeh pareshaani, kiske pati ne apni biwi chudwayi yeh pareshaani,

Salo to kare-to-kare kya

Kabhi kabhi lagta hai Bhagwan ne sex maje ke liye banaya tha ya pareshaaniyo ke liye."

Translation

"Happiness and all problems of Indians are connected to sex

They have problem with rape

They have problem with incest

They have problem with child abuse

They have problem with polygamy

This is all fine, why Aishwairya Rai (actor) didn't become a mother? They have problem if couples divorce,

Buddies, what else to do? Sometimes I wonder whether God created sex for fun or to create problems."

"All these modern philosophies of sexual freedom are products of western consumer culture."

"Goodness has nothing to change and that what is not good will not survive."

"Some say, if homosexuality is normal, then why is it practiced by so few? The great majority of people are heterosexual."

"Are they 'more' normal?"

"Homosexuality existed in India since hundreds of years ago (or even more). Why did our ancestors did not value "love" between two human beings more than just populating the world?"

16

Homophobia

"Homophobia displayed by straight people is one thing, but we ourselves are no better, why blame others when we ourselves discriminate people of our community go to any gay party and you'll see this even take these forums for example so many personal attacks by fellow gay men why blame the outsiders."

"I am told, man should not act like woman."

"Be happy that they don't think that being gay is equal to being eunuch because 5 years back most of the straights did think like this."

17
Filmy Romance

"Bas yahi apraadh har baar karta hun... Aadmi hun aadmi se pyar karta hun... (That's the only crime I do everytime, love man)."

"Hum hain rahi pyar ke, hamse kuch na boliye, Jo bhi pyar se mila, Hum usi ke ho liye..." (We are travelers of love, don't say anything to us, whoever met with love, we belong to him)."

"Yeh dosti, hum nahi chodenge...." (We will not break this friendship)."

"In the olden days homosexuality was symbolically depicted in movies.... because of the taboo attached to it, in most movies, the hero and the side hero used to be such langotia yaaars, (buddies) that they used hug and almost kiss each other, the dialogues used to be loaded with symbolism, about how they loved each other..."

"Chahunga Mein Tujhe Shaam Savere, Phir Bhi Kabhi Ab Naam Ko Tere." (I will love you day and night, yet sometimes now the name of yours I will not give voice; I will not give voice) from the black & white film *Dosti*.

"In fact, I could feel such strong homosexual currents going on between the two friends."

"In that film, one friend says to the other blind friend, 'Tumhare hoth kitne ache hain' (Your lips are so beautiful)."

"And then, one more song from Sangam, 'Dost Dost Na Raha, Pyaar Pyaar Na Raha' (Friend no more, love no more)."

"My first lover used to sing this song whenever I refused to let him kiss me and he wanted to taunt me in front of others."

"*Dosti* is a landmark film.... It's about two teenage friends ...there was no heroine in the film...

If I remember well...the Langada friend (disabled friend) tells the Blind one 'Tumhari Ankhen kitni Khoobsurat hai' (yours eyes are so beautiful)..to which the Blind says 'Par kis kam ki' (but what's the use)."

"Every time I saw the film, I had my eyes flooded...it's a very touching film, well directed."

"The film had no lead female character. The film had no conscious homosexual vibe exchanged by the two, but just that, I kind of read all that...........I mean throughout the film the two friends feel for each other just the way lovers would feel for each other. Wahi sab, impress karna, friendship karna, ruthna, manana, (same way how couples impress, explore each other while doing that they sometimes get anger sometimes they persuade the other with love etc.) and look at the wordings of the song 'Chahunga mein tujhe...' (I will love you) I mean, sounds more like a song that a person would sing for his lover than for a friend."

"It could be that the director of the film deliberately hesitated to bring out the homosexual content in the film due to the stigma or shame attached to the subject. Moreover, same-sex sexuality was never spoken."

18

Gay World

"It's all stereotypism."

"There is only one world where we all humans live. ...I don't know despite being extensive media coverage about homosexuality why do people still categorize humans?"

"I hate it when people say stuff like 'in the gay world this' and 'in the gay world that' Is it really all that different from the real world, or the so-called straight world? Acche bure log toh har jagah hote hain (Good and bad people exist at every place)."

References

Andree Robinson-Neal, Academic writing can be an art, but the process is like a sport, THE PRESS ENTERPRISE, May 13, 2020.

Margaret K. Merga, Shannon Mason, Mentor and peer support for early career researchers sharing research with academia and beyond, Heliyon, 2021.

Margaret Merga, Shannon Mason, Early career researchers' perceptions of the benefits and challenges of sharing research with academic and non-academic end-users, Higher Education Research & Development, 2020.

Olshansky, Beth. Making Writing a Work of Art: Image-Making Within the Writing Process. Language Arts, Vol. 71, September 1994.

Pamela Burnard, Elizabeth Mackinlay, et. al., Doing Rebellious Research: In and Beyond the Academy, Brill, 2022.

Patrick Dunleavy & Jane Tinkler. Maximizing the impacts of Academic Research, Bloomsbury Publishing, 2020.

Schäfer, Elisabeth. "WRITING AS ARTISTIC RESEARCH". Teaching Artistic Research: Conversations Across Cultures, edited by Ruth Mateus-Berr and Richard Jochum, Berlin, Boston: De Gruyter, 2020.

www.ingramcontent.com/pod-product-compliance
Lightning Source LLC
Chambersburg PA
CBHW071240140726
47996CB00007B/2690